RELEASE THE WISDOM IN YOU

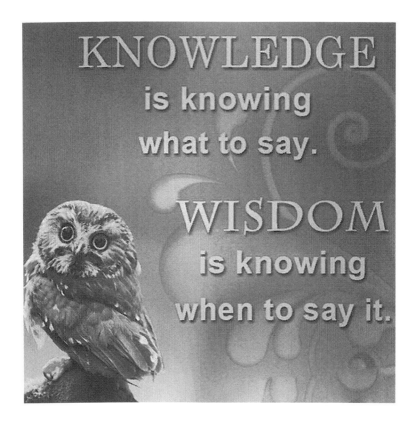

KNOWLEDGE
is knowing
what to say.

WISDOM
is knowing
when to say it.

MAGELLA DUHAIME

TABLE OF CONTENT

INTRODUCTION

"Release The Wisdom in You". I found comes from our inner self anytime and anywhere. The world is your reality by your own thoughts. One thing I found amazing when one thinks of the past or future isn't that also your present thinking.

This time around I wanted to share with my readers my spiritual journey. I have included examples with names for my guides that were put into place to make it more real. We sometimes take for granted those that have given us a helping hand.

My spiritual journey has brought me to a place of calmness that is not so worrisome. First, I had to believe that I do have a Higher Power. Then I am not alone. Those that seek Him will be eternally happy and humble.

Many years have gone by, and searching was my mission to try to be happy and at peace with myself.

I am sharing with you my experience that placed me on this path. Hopefully you will receive some knowledge of how it's done.

My prayers for all. "Dear Lord, help me spread your fragrance wherever I am. Use your love to give them peace and happiness. "We are all designed to bring out the best of each other." Help me walk in love.

Those that are familiar with the Wizard of Oz when Dorothy says I want to go home. She didn't even have to leave her home to find out she had everything she needed in her own backyard. "Herself".

(Romans 12:2 Be not conformed to this world. But be ye transformed by the renewing of your mind, that ye may prove what is that is good, and acceptable and perfect will of God.

ACKNOWLEDGEMENT

I would like to give a big thanks to my sister, Angela, who always has my back. If it wasn't for her encouragement, I don't believe I would have gotten this far for my third book. She is my editor and knows me better than I know myself at times. I rely on her views in pursuing my goals on giving understanding to my messages for others to help on their spiritual journey

I have also several great friends and family that I surround myself with. I consider them as my confidants. A big thanks for putting me up with me through my spiritual journey. My school buddies Betty and Donna. My Bible Study friends June, Bernie, Bunny, Beverly.

MEMORY TO MY FATHER

Most of all I want to give a tribute to my father. I have been very fortunate to have doors open for me. My father would tell me hard work will make you emotionally stronger no matter who you encounter. Not to let others think they're smarter than you because they are not. Everyone has a job to do on this planet, that's it. His example of a protector and provider showed me the responsibility of having a family.

There was no room for debating what is right or wrong. He had four girls and always taught us of having independent thought. Not to settle anything less or bargain your morals for something to make you less than your own worth.

God Bless you Dad

ABOUT THE AUTHOR

Magella Duhaime resides in North Carolina. This is her third book and would like to share with her readers the process so far on her life's journey. There was a time when I thought what more information, I would come across that enlightens those that have been following me.

It's one thing to have tools given by other authors that enhance their journey. We need to apply them to our own success. Along with the practice in itself.

Each and every one of us has a self-talk in us. We have also been given choices. To either listen or not. Never give your power away to others.

In "Release the Wisdom in You" is a reminder to be generous monetary, but to share our knowledge of kindness and compliments to others. The greatest gift giving is to find common ground in everyone.

(2 Corinthians 3:18)

But we all know, with an unveiled face, beholding as in a mirror, "The glory of the Lord are being transformed into the same image from glory to glory, just as the Spirit of the Lord.

CHAPTER 1

THE START OF MY SPIRITUAL JOURNEY

Experience the Lord:

May 1996

I feel it's time to share with you my experience with the Lord. Back in 1996 I left
Massachusetts for North Carolina. I was
in a dilemma I lost my home, business,
marriage on the rocks. I needed to make a
change. It's really something when I finally,
I had my family help and friends whereas
before they tried, I just wasn't ready.

I received a call from my previous employer that the office manager
position was available. I accepted it for the time being. Unfortunately,
it wasn't what I had expected.

Before I left, I took a ride to where I was brought up to see it for the last
time. There was a reservoir where I sat looking over the calm waters,
between my tears I said to Him "Dear Lord, I need you now more than
ever." Please show me a sign.

After that experience I drove away. The next day I came to work to finish my notice. I talked to Lorraine she was the locker room attendant. I told her what I did at the reservoir and cried my eyes out. Lorraine told me to explain that moment and I told her. Her reply she said, "The Lord has you." That your writings and speeches let Him work through you. You're the Lord's Instrument.

Looking back and understanding it's all in the timing (not mine) it's the Lord's I truly believe that.

Since then that I noticed the Lord comes in all forms.

I was moved by my writings, and this is how I was guided.

This was my first piece of writing in 1996.

Thank you, Lorraine.

One night I was talking with the Lord,

I said to Him so your my Boss!!

No Paycheck, no nothing

His reply was your're right!

You mean to tell me all the bosses I have had was you all along.

He Answered ~you're right!!

All my mentors I have had to this point.

It was you?

Correct.

Oh My God!!
You're right again.

Matthew 25:14-30 Story to explain scatter than gather.

The Parable of the Talents

"For the *kingdom of heaven is* like a man traveling to a far country, *who* called his own servants and delivered his goods to them. And to one he gave five talents, to another two, and to another one, to each according to his own ability; and immediately he went on a journey. Then he who had received the five talents went and traded with them and made another five talents. And likewise, he who *had received* two gained two more also. But he who had received one went and dug in the ground and hid his lord's money. After a long time the lord of those servants came and settled accounts with them.

"So, he who had received five talents came and brought five other talents, saying, 'Lord, you delivered to me five talents; look, I have gained five more talents besides them.' His lord said to him, 'Well *done*, good and faithful servant; you were faithful over a few things, I will make you ruler over many things. Enter into the joy of your lord.' He also who had received two talents came and said, 'Lord, you delivered to me two talents; look, I have gained two more talents besides them.' His lord said to him, 'Well *done*, good and faithful servant; you have been faithful over a few things, I will make you ruler over many things. Enter into the joy of your lord.'

"Then he who had received the one talent came and said, 'Lord, I knew you to be a hard man, reaping where you have not sown, and gathering where you have not scattered seed. And I was afraid and went and hid your talent in the ground. Look, *there* you have *what is* yours.'

"But his lord answered and said to him, 'You wicked and lazy servant, you knew that I reap where I have not sown and gather where I have not scattered seed. So, you ought to have deposited my money with the bankers, and at my coming I would have received back my own with interest. So, take the talent from him, and give *it* to him who has ten talents.

'For to everyone who has, more will be given, and he will have abundance; but from him who does not have, even what he has will be taken away. And cast the unprofitable servant into the outer darkness. There will be weeping and gnashing of teeth.'

I do believe the Lord has plans to sprinkle in people with their gifts and talents to provide helping others in the process. That our society would be more joyful. Everyday should be happy. We all have choices in life. Be accountable for your own gifts. Your path will reveal itself. "Seek and you shall find."

It is a process. Sometimes it will take a while to practice baby steps. Watch for guides that the Lord has placed in your life. In can be from people, books, movies, songs be open to the experiences. Welcome your days even if it's mundane. Make those times extraordinary by being creative. God does not demand that you be successful. God demands that you are faithful is what is important.

"There are times I question myself. "What does is mean to be a disciple of the Lord?" I am reminded in Proverbs 3:5-6 King James Version 5 Trust in the Lord with all thine heart; and lean not unto thine own understanding. In all thy ways acknowledge him, and he shall direct thy paths.

CHAPTER 2

AN INCREDIBLY SPECIAL RELATIONSHIP IS ONE IN A LIFETIME.

KINDRED SOUL
ANGEL ENCOUNTERS
Exodus 23:20

"Behold I send an Angel before you to keep you in the way and to bring you into the place which I have prepared."

Kindred Souls refers to someone with whom you share a strong connection due to similar tastes, thoughts, feelings, or temperament. It's a like-minded person with whom you feel an instant rapport or deep bond. The phrase implies finding a rare, special connection with someone who understands you profoundly due to a similarity in spirit or life experiences.

The first time I heard that term, was Nana. She was a grandmother on my husband's side, I would take her to places that she loved, going to card shops, bookstores and we would have lunch. I also enjoyed it myself. She was known for being late, I would pick her up at noon. It always amazed me she was on time dressed, hair comb kerchiefs so her hair wouldn't mess up.

She would always tell me Magella, we are just kindred spirits. Like minded folks.

Special relationships should be treasured and make one feel you can be you. Through thick and thin. You can always count on a good friend. Maybe we should go back.

"Pinky Swear" To cement the relationship.

(Proverbs 17:27-28)

"He who has knowledge spares his words. And a man of understanding is of a calm spirit. Even a fool is counted wise when he holds his peace. When he shuts his lips, he is considered perceptive.

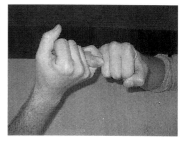

True friendship isn't about being inseparable it's being separated and nothing changes.

CHAPTER 3

BLESSINGS FROM GOD IS A MIRACLE

CREATIONS

So, God created man in his own image, in the image of God created he him; male and female created he them, (Gen:1:27) Jeremiah (1:4-5)

Then the word of the Lord came unto me saying, "Before I formed thee in the belly I knew thee; and before thou camest forth out of the womb I sanctioned thee, and I ordained thee prophet unto the nations.

The baby in a mother's womb should be celebrated. Never forget the Lord will not give us anything we cannot handle. For He will equip those that seek a blessing from Him.

Imagine billions of people all different from each other with their own unique gifts and talents. Be accountable for sharing those gifts to others in the Lord's purpose.

Each one of us has different make up. Babies are the most precious. They are miracles of God's Blessings. God's given gifts.

There was a time when I questioned why I was born. Being at the end of a raging mother would slap me around to discipline me. I thought to myself, "what did I do wrong? She wouldn't stop. Till years later. I debated with people saying that was an effective way to keep a child in line. Well in my view it wasn't the case for me.

As a child I would think to myself that someday I would be bigger than her and see how she would like it. One really needs to consider raising children is a tremendous responsibility.

Children are the best examples and should be cherished for every action they take. Adults can learn from them. I love honesty and innocence. Please remember it is easier to build a strong child than to repair a broken man. Their behavior is so innocent and pure.

Like flowers, or snowflakes in every aspect, nature at its best. How one cannot admit there must have been someone higher than us to create such brilliance.

I look at trees.... blades of grass.... flowers blooming.... The sound of ocean waves floating back and forth. As hard as many tries to create what we have, and they will never surpass There are times when one should take the time God given gifts. It's just the way it's intended to be.

No one can compete for such brilliance than God.

In the prayer Our Father: Your kingdom come; your will be done on earth as it is in heaven.

CHAPTER 4

YOU ARE JUST ONE DECISION AWAY.

Run your own race. It's not the cup. It's the coffee.

The idea that we have the power to change our lives with a single decision. Meaning you have the power to take ownership of your life making intentional choices that align with our values and goals.

It reminds us that even small decisions can have a significant impact and that we should not be afraid to take risks or try new things. A reminder that we are in control and have the power to shape our future.

Unfortunately, people do not show the courage to take a path-breaking decision because their past experiences don't justify that. Never think that you wasted all past days. The past is the past and you cannot take it back.

The biggest decision for me was to leave my marriage and start a new life. They were years it took me to finally say enough. I have done whatever I could with no satisfaction. Include with results came out of that situation. Once I made up my mind my heart said the same thing. What happened everything fell into place. I thank the Lord for that.

Everyone deserves self-respect and not to give our power to others that don't respect you. It's a process to achieve a bit in time, it gets easier. Once you can feel uncomfortable in certain situations that doesn't agree with your moral beliefs time to take the walk,

Someone had told me when praying to be more specific about requesting help. We all know of someone who needs a hand up and there is nothing we could have done. It's their choice. One of my favorite scriptures explains the exact situation.

Do not be misled by bad character company that corrupts bad character. No more arguing with people who don't align with each other.

Psalm 142-2

When my spirit was overwhelmed within me, then thou knowest my path, in the way wherein I walked have privily laid a snare for me.

Psalm 143-3

For the enemy half persecuted my soul: he smitten my life down to the ground he hath, as those that have been long dead.

Translated to Mean:

He had cried out to the Lord and the Lord filled him with his spirit and he was saved and living by the Lord.

So, his friends in the past were not his refuge because he always had wickedness on their mind and would do, maybe using him encouraging him to drink or do drugs anything worldly like a snake in the grass.

The only way to make sense of change is to plunge into it, move with it and join the dance.

At times people will cross your path and be aware of them. Interesting to note how they cast their own energy towards you. Sometimes good, other times not so good. Try to stay away from negativity.

I read at one time that really struck me. We do not need to be a wishbone we need to have a backbone. Courageous people will press until they find out more knowledge about what to seek. We are all one race, the human race. There is nothing wrong with being exceptional. We are all special.

CHAPTER 5

MEANING OF FIRE IN THE BELLY

"Do it and do it right even if you are alone do not comprise."

Aspirations:

Have you ever wondered about daydreaming about what you would like to become or conduct?

A yearning to conduct goals to succeed.

Fire in the Belly: A desire to learn or know constantly searching for more information on your desire. In other words, the emotion, passion, or inner drive to achieve something to act.

I always wanted to be a writer. In high school I was in business classes. I loved my bookkeeping class so much I thought back about pursuing as an accountant. I was transferred to an English class I always had a problem where to put commas, and grammar etc.

Her reply to me, you will never be a writer. Voila, here I am an Author. When at that time I thought it would never be possible.

For me I started writing in a journal had a friend make a little book The Awakening. I still have one of the copies left. That year I had mailed them to my friends and family as Christmas Gifts. My younger sister gave me $10.00 for that piece of work. Publishers were so expensive. Years went by and today it is so much cheaper and easier. Looking back today it was all in His timing (not mine). Might not happen right away. I have concluded that there is a life lesson that needs to be learnt. There is a saying if you love what you do it's not a job. When that happens you not only enjoy but your knowledge of the tasks increasing your gifts, and talents for others.

Someone asked me "How will I know mine? Anything that makes you happy and loving. A simple smile and kind gestures which is given to you by our Creator. If our society were open to love and happiness maybe we could go there, for starters.

(Luke 9-1)
Define what's in your heart he called them hear the calling. God doesn't call people who are equipped He equips them for his calling. When you struggle only means you have a draw need to be open by God.

When someone says I would like to be a sky diver the answer is not you will never be one. The reply should be to take these steps and tools to achieve your dream.

Asking questions like what gives you the drive or energy to get up in the mornings? A drive to look forward to your day. Stick your toe in the water. "Dream Big" "Start Small" Baby steps make you feel confident. That you conducted a task then on to the next one. Pretty soon you are on top of the elevator. Constantly bear in mind that information you need for your dreams. Take advantage of people who are more experienced and have succeeded. Stop complaining about your competitors and learn from them.

Enjoy every step of the way in your life's journey.

CHAPTER 6

CAPTAIN OF YOUR OWN SHIP

Use your own creativity rather than someone else's.

Find your own calling in the Lord's will.

(Proverbs 4:7) Wisdom is the principal thing, get wisdom and with all thy getting get understanding.

Let us all be the heads of our mouths. So, you will not be slaves to your words.

Master your emotions. A calm mind can manage any situation.

You need to be smart enough to create your opportunities, do not wait for them to come to you.

Steer in the direction of what gives you joy. People like to gravitate to those that have that kind of energy. Be aware of them and realize you are the one that creates it. Be grateful for all humanity.

Do not give anyone your power. In other words, control your emotions. Do not be baited.

When one walks confidently it is attractive. Not in a physical sense. But a sense of reassuring that (he or she) knows exactly what they want. One knows they are their own Captain. No questions asked.

Discovering those hidden talents would be amazing.

Being a writer means to me doing something that will have an effect and understanding that I have a choice whether to do it or not. I have developed self-awareness about getting that done. I am the Captain of my Ship.

(Matthew 6:19-21)
Do not store up for yourselves treasures on earth, where moths and vermin destroy, and where thieves break in and steal. But lay up for yourselves treasures in heaven. For where your treasures there your heart there will be also. (Matthew 6-6) Be careful not to practice to your righteousness in front of others to be seen by them. If you do, you will have no reward from your Father in heaven.

CHAPTER 7

OPERATING UNDER A NEW LENS

Getting out of an old way of thinking.

Do not project to others with the lens of your past experiences.

When you operate from a happy lens. Then when someone approaches you the reaction is amazing.

The moral of the story: A woman was complaining about her neighbor's wash drying on the line kept saying she has dirty laundry. One morning she woke up and the laundry was spanking clean. She told her husband and said I do not know what happened to her laundry looks great. Her husband replied later in the day I washed your windows. Now that is a lesson for everyone to work under a different lens.

One gets empathy when you experience having trouble in the past to relate makes one understand another shortcoming. Put yourself in their shoes.

Makes one less judgmental.

Do not be afraid of making mistakes. Own up to it and dust yourself off and move on. The greatest philosophers and inventors learn from their own mistakes and have evolved to share with us their wisdom for a better society.

The best thing I heard when someone admits to their faults and says, "This was the old me and now this is the new me." I didn't know then, but I do know now.

When the Lord guides you, He gives you a little nudge, then no response He will give you another push. When thoughts coming from you create anger. It's time to know the reason why.

Comparison by having your eyes corrected by a vision lens. The clarity will be so different than before. I have just gotten hearing aids and cannot believe how much I was missing in conversations with my family and friends.

It's taking on a new perspective in my life's journey. It enhances one's thought process also. Which will allow you to look at someone's ideas that might be different than yours. Then the conversation can be calm without the emotions created and able to open to an intelligent sharing of different views.

CHAPTER 8

WALK THE TALK ~ TAKE THE MASK OFF.

Everyone will show you who they are, just give them time.

Try to reach a common ground not a middle ground.

Taking off one's mask can be incredibly challenging. Pretending you are someone that you are not than being oneself is playing deceitful game. It is better to be honest than lead others to believe the deceitful game you project. In other words, you will attract those that think you are someone you are not.

I find being congruent in mind and soul. Which means having your thoughts coincide with your heart. Makes you confident of the real you. A real person. Plus, it will create you not to be torn on how to act. You are who you are, I am what I am. I am Popeye the sailor girl.

I was naïve on this front. I would take people for their own words. Constantly being disappointed they turned out lying. That's a fact. On top of that I would cover their behavior. Thinking no they wouldn't do that. Till one day I realized that is just how the cookie crumbles. It is true "actions speak louder than words".

Have you ever been in a situation where you have been vulnerable to a person then come to find out they use your weakness to either tell others or confront you reminding you of the story you had just shared with them. Years ago, I had to learn that lesson. My sister had reminded me to wait for the other person reveal themselves do not spill my guts out first. Solved that problem really quick.

(Proverbs 20:19)
He that goeth about as a talebearer revealeth secrets: there-fore, meddle not with him that flattereth with his lips.
(Philippians' 3:16)
Nevertheless, to the degree that we have already attained "let us walk by the same "rule" let us be of the same mind.

CHAPTER 9

BEING IN A MATURE SPIRITUAL RELATIONSHIP

Master your emotions. A calm mind can manage any situation.

If you want to do better, be better.

The lessons will keep appearing till you learn that lesson. Do not be a repeater especially in a loving relationship. One thing I learnt everything I think is not the same for everyone.

Remember the day we first started talking to each other?

'Cause that's what started you and I.

There was a time that we would use the term loving relationship frankly I haven't heard that word used any longer. My opinion of that is people are missing the whole emotional ties experience it's the most exhilarating feeling when a couple connects with each other a part of my hand, the softness of a kiss, caressing each other in a loving way. Frankly, what I see today is people even in the movies are acting like animals. Where is the emotional ties? In my day we will yet to be engaged which meant to get to know one another dating going out as a couple talk about ourselves and enjoying each other's company. A long time falling in love, music was for lovers with the country singers, soul singers, easy listening were heartfelt sadly there are not enough of it how do we instruct our children if not by example? My father always gave my mother a kiss and a hug, I would watch and felt so much comfort and safety he was the protector of the family and didn't let us down.

Sitting back and just watching their character is not a bad idea.

Take time to look into their eyes, does it really stand for their souls? Do you see happiness or sadness?

Let us bring back words with respect, sincerity, and honesty. No one should have the upper hand over each other.

The term battle of the sexes should be gone. Equality is achieved when male and female know their roles by enhancing each other's strengths and weakness. There is no room for constantly competing.

No more complaints. Skip the blame game. Stay calm. Skip arguments. Stay humble. Learn to listen. Talk later.

Maturity recognizes they do not play games. Honesty and straightforward. Don't depend on one another for happiness. Confident, mature women and men neglect don't hold grudges and are forgiving of one another. Understanding. Easy and resilient and persist. I notice with women and men coming out of a bad situation how many carry that baggage not even knowing how they project to others. Who did it affect the person that loves you the most.

In Bible Study they mentioned. The cross was the most holy act of Forgiveness that ever took place.

Mark 11:25 - And when ye stand praying, forgive, if ye have fought against any: that your Father also which is in heaven may forgive you your trespasses. Ephesians 4:32 - And be ye kind one to another, tenderhearted, forgiving one another, even as God for Christ's sake hath forgiven you.

It was just a relief to me that I did overcome it.

CHAPTER 10

PAY IT FORWARD

With your generosity. Thinking for someone else besides you.

Jesus sends us people in all forms to Pay It Forward can mean that one uses his or her gifts and talents to help others in their dire need. Just as the Lord intended it to be.

(Matthew 6:17-18)
But when you fast anoint your head and wash your face. So that you do not appear to man to be fasting but to your father who is in the secret place and your father who sees in secret will reward you openly.
(Matthew 7: 7-8)
Ask and it will be given to you seek and you will find knock and it will open to you. For everyone who asks receives.

There will be times when one must have faith that when receiving will be more than expected by the Lord's way not yours. Just experience and welcome the gifts.

When approached with the kindness of people be so grateful it is the Lord's working through them.

There is no coincidence. We have a place to leave and take table. Many times, I was looking for a small coffee pot, or a purse, some as trivial as that. And voila!! Appeared to me at the right time. You would be surprised how many times in your journey that happened to you and is taken for granted. These are the times to take notice and be grateful. For the Lord's blessings.

CHAPTER 11

MY GOD IS LOVING AND CARING

"God doesn't demand that I be successful. God demands that I am faithful is what is more important.

Be accountable for your inner self

There are times one goes through battles thinking there is no way out. I haven't met one person that hasn't been affected. It's up to you to make the choice sit back and moan or rise and survive. Keep in mind the world doesn't revolve around you.

Today I rely on my faith to get me through the good and tough times. First, it keeps me humble knowing a Higher Power will be there. Takes the pressure off. It's very enlightening and calming.

We mirror each other. If you are operating in a loving way you will find others with the same outlook. Pity does that walk-through life with hate, and anger. They are wasting so much time and energy. It also reflects in their negativity as physical beings

The Lord's plan is to have everyone strive to be happy.

Bear in mind, keep your emotions in check. Set an example for our children. It's not ok to throw a temper tantrum. Practice makes perfect.

(1 Corinthians 13:4-7)

Love is patient, love is kind and is not jealous; love does not brag and is not arrogant, does not act unbecomingly; it does not seek its own, is not provoked, does not rejoice a wrong suffered, does not rejoice in unrighteousness, but rejoices with the truth.

CHAPTER 12

EXPERIENCE THE EXPERIENCES.

Meaning to enjoy experiences. At times looking back it was the memory that is important. Either way one gained more knowledge of the outcomes. Relish it and put it as a memory to be talked about for years to come.

When my grandchildren came along, I realized how great it was to be their grandmother. I can sit back and spoil them. Loved every minute of it. I showered them with love, fun and laughter. Happiness is the key to having a "Do Over. 'Sometimes in our life journeys we tend to forget that living in the moment can be so precious.

Children are better than some adults in their own little world. Resilient and bouncing back is so much easier than adults.

When one is at a place that is out of your comfort zone. Which do you choose to handle that particular situation. It can be a welcome experience just by your own thinking. You have the power to decide. Most of the time we expect more and become disappointed by our own expectations. Suddenly our emotions get involved also. I practice taking a breath, relaxing in the experiences till it subsides. It will happen. As my stepmother would say "This too will past". Best advice I received.

(Hebrew 6:25)

The Lord makes His face shine upon you. And be gracious to you. "The Lord lift up his countenance you and give you peace."

CHAPTER 13

IT'S ALL IN HIS TIMING

Lord, what is my agenda today?

God will replace your friends with others have faith in Him.

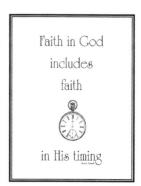

Faith in God
includes
faith
in His timing

Life is so much easier when I allow my faith and just let the Lord take over at times. Why fight it? It only resolves in making me angry at the world. Plus, my energy is not up to par with others. I rather be calm and leave the situation.

Cool and collective.

I have found a great Bible Study group. At first, I just thought I would try it. The moment I walked in I found it very welcoming and energetic. I usually go by my gut should I stay or should I go. I took my seat. I learnt so much that night about the Bible. I heard people saying I read the whole book. I found it not like reading a novel. That answered that. Bible study gives a translation of the scripture applying in today's world.

The Bible is a correction with direction.

Read Have a Good Bible Study to translate.
Study The more you study the more you gain.
Practice Live by the Word
Doer. Learn by humility.

When I say it's all in His timing, I feel no stress or anxiety when I can do my best and if not in my own timing, I say to myself it is the Lord's. No more trying to be Ms. Fixer. I have this idea when I see things go awry my old self would want to fix it. Most of the time it wasn't working anyway.

(Mark 11:24)

"Therefore, I say to you whatever things you ask when you pray, believe that you receive them, and you will have them."

CHAPTER 14

DEFINE WHO YOU ARE!!!

Make a Contract to Oneself

Be careful what you wish for. "Think little will get you little".

The way we treat people is the way we treat Jesus.

Years ago, I had attended a seminar and was told to improve my thought process by being more positive. In one segment they had us write a contract to ourselves in how we would be portraying to others. They circled me and asked what I thought of who I truly aim. In tears I said, "I am a loving, caring and beautiful woman." They had me write it out on a huge page and sign my name. Has anyone taken the time to say to themselves how do I walk this planet" I took my contract and had framed it. Today I can truly say "Yeah I am." I still remember that experience on my life's path.

(Phil: 4-11)
Not that I speak in regard to need, for I have learned to whatever state I am into be content.
(Romans 15:5-8)
"Now may the God of patience and comfort grant you to like-minded toward one another, according to Christ Jesus. That you may with one mouth glorify the God and Father or

our Lord Jesus Christ. Therefore receive one another just "as Christ also received us to the glory of God.

I am a work in progress. Knowing more than before. And anxious to learn more.

CHAPTER 15

"LET NOT YOUR HEART BE TROUBLE."

To gain respect, be honest.

It starts in the home and our communities. Growing up my father taught me honesty is the best policy.

He had an experience at work where I saw him telling the truth about the accident he had at the shop. Apparently, there were a couple of young people that pushed him into a cut up barrel at the furniture shop. Cut up his back and as he was leaving there were others that saw what happened and told him not to worry, they would vouch for my father in order to collect worker's compensation. When it came time to have the witness no one showed up. The insurance agent had recorded his story. I watched my father in tears but stood his ground. He was declined the insurance. Never once did he lie about the situation.

He told me he would never lie to anyone or lie for anyone.

When one is in congruent with self. It's very clear to know the right thing, Say the right thing, and do the right thing. Therefore, it relieves the anxious feeling, or being torn of what to do. It's very freeing of your own moral compass.

Being committed to honesty. Will always make you sincere and respected.

(Proverbs 11:3)
The integrity of the upright will guide them. But the perversity of the unfaithful will destroys them.

(1 Peter 5:7)
Cast in all your cares upon Him for He cares for you.

CHAPTER 16

I AM MY OWN TRAVEL AGENT IN LIFE.

Your mind is your power within.

(Isaih 55:8)
"For my thoughts are not your thoughts. Nor are your ways, my ways say the Lord".
(Romans 12:2)
And be not conformed to this world: but be ye transformed by the renewing of your mind, that ye may prove what is that good, and acceptable, and perfect, will of God.

Honor the small things experiences the present moments. Remember thoughts of the past or future is really the present and can be addressed in your own mind. You have the power of the switch to turn it on and off.

Be optimistic rather than not. It's entirely possible to override the feelings. You decide. Don't wait for a time of celebration, create your own on a daily basis. Allow yourself to being a travel agent for your destiny. Make a practice of saying to yourself before you start your day something good is going to happen today.

When confronted with negativity keep emotions in check do not be allowed to be baited in the same posture as those trying to affect a response.

CHAPTER 17

THE MEANING OF EPIPHANY

ENLIGHTMENT – A DIVINE EXPERIENCE

Signifies a sudden realization or a flash of Recognition where someone's thinking Seeing a revelation of insight.

The lesson will always repeat itself. Until you learn the lesson. Have you ever wondered why you are attracted to a particular person and are not very respectful towards you? Say to yourself why do I always end up in the same boat with a leak. When I started to look inward,

I found my answer and I no longer take the time to change them, I change myself.

(Romans 12-23) Do not conform any longer to the patter of this world but be transformed by renewing your mind.

I can share the tools that I found for myself then it's time for one to pick up the baton and find your own spiritual path to love and happiness.

When I realized I had a mission one of them is to find out how does one go about such a pursuit.

I attended meetings for co-dependent anonymous it is based on a 12-step program. I really didn't pay all that much for saying it. Unfortunately, I mentioned it to someone and recalled him saying it is all in his timing.

I will share my tools that made me evolve spiritually. The Serenity Prayer, I have repeated it and finally got the message.

THE TWELVE STEPS PROGRAM IS VERY CHRISTIAN BASED FOR ME: I would like to expand to others this prayer can be for anyone struggling from any addictions.

When someone does not have control of there own lifestyle time to find the reasons why and address it promptly. It's not acceptable to harm oneself or others.

We admitted we were powerless over alcohol or drugs that our lives had become unmanageable.

Came to believe that Power greater than ourselves could restore us to sanity.

Made a decision to turn our will and our lives over to the care of God as we understood Him.

Made a searching and fearless moral inventory of ourselves.

Admitted to God to ourselves and to another human being the exact nature of our wrong doings.

Were entirely ready to have God remove all these defects of character

Humbly asked Him to remove our shortcomings.

Made a list of all the people we had harmed and became willing to make amends to all.

Made direct amends to such people wherever possible, expect when doing so would injure them or others. Continued to take personal inventory and when we were wrong promptly admitted it.

Sought through prayer and meditation to improve and conscious contact with Him.

Having had a spiritual awakening as the result of these steps, we tried to carry this message to all addicts to practice these principles in all our affairs.

My best tool and no other are finding a bible study group, church. That preach the bible precisely as it is written. There are a lot of experts. My personal preference is Joyce Meyers, C.S. Lewis, Les Feldick. Reminding you seek and you will find what fits for you.

I also would like to mention at times I found myself in the process of books I never understood, and I would keep them either I like the cover or the title. One time I met a woman and the conversation was about a book called The Handbook of Higher Consciousness I replied to her I didn't quite understand what the author meant. She said read it now you will so I did and I understood. It's all in His timing, that's all I can say. Do not be discouraged in searching for more information. You will find to be thirsty for more.

Life is like a puzzle
only He can put the puzzle
together because we don't have a
picture to go by. He knows how
because He's the one that
made the puzzle.

God Bless You
My Friend
Junebug

THE BEST INSTUCTION BOOK
THE BIBLE

GOD BLESS
&
AMEN

Made in the USA
Columbia, SC
07 December 2024

47630075R00031